THE OFFICIAL itv SPORT
CHAMPIONS LEAGUE
ANNUAL 2009

Written by Pete Oliver

GRANADA

Ventures

The ITV Sport logo is licensed by Granada Ventures Ltd.

All rights reserved.

A Grange Publication

© 2008. Published by Grange Communications Ltd., Edinburgh, under licence from Granada Ventures Ltd. Printed in the EU.

Photographs © Action Images

ISBN 978-1-906211-68-4

£6.99

Roll of Honour

Manchester United's dramatic triumph in the 2008 Champions League final made the Old Trafford club kings of Europe for the third time in their history.

United won the European Cup at Wembley in 1968 and then lifted the Champions League crown at Barcelona's Camp Nou Stadium in 1999.

Since the European Cup, which was won for the first time in 1956 by Spanish giants Real Madrid, became the Champions League in 1992/93, only three clubs have won it twice or more.

United's win over Chelsea saw them join AC Milan and Real Madrid on the list of Europe's elite.

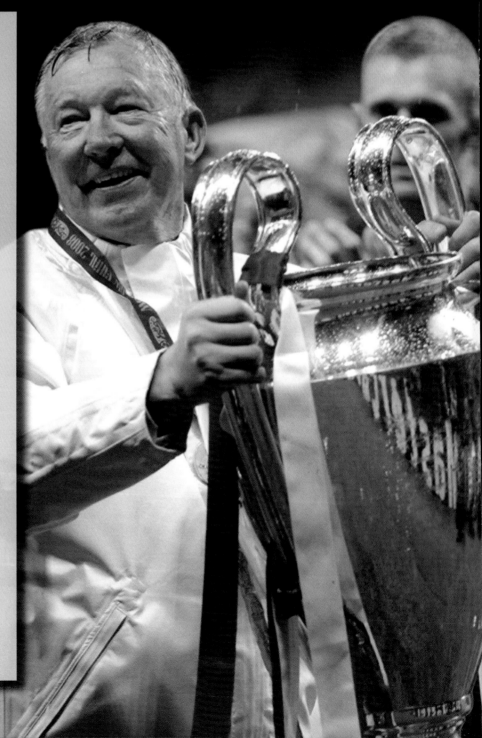

CHAMPIONS LEAGUE WINNERS

2007/08 Manchester United

2006/07 AC Milan

2005/06 Barcelona

2004/05 Liverpool

2003/04 FC Porto

2002/03 AC Milan

2001/02 Real Madrid

2000/01 Bayern Munich

1999/00 Real Madrid

1998/99 Manchester United

1997/98 Real Madrid

1996/97 Borussia Dortmund

1995/96 Juventus

1994/95 Ajax

1993/94 AC Milan

1992/93 Olympique de Marseille

Contents

Introduction

Well, what a year that was. The 2007/08 Champions League season took British football to new heights as the Premier League claimed a stranglehold on Europe.

Three of the four semi-finalists all came from our league, producing a classic final between Chelsea and Manchester United.

And who could forget that epic clash on a rain-soaked night in Moscow when United claimed the title in the most dramatic of penalty shoot-outs?

ITV Sport was delighted to bring you all the thrills, spills, goals, glory, agony and ecstasy that started out with the cream of Europe battling through the group stages to culminate in Alex Ferguson's side completing a repeat of their famous 1999 double.

ITV's extensive coverage also brought you the successes of Celtic and Rangers and our commitment to covering the world's top clubs in European competition

means we will continue to show the best Champions League matches.

And who's year will it be in 2008/09? Can United maintain their grip on the trophy, will Chelsea finally conquer Europe, can Liverpool get it right at home and abroad, will Arsène Wenger land the big prize he wants for Arsenal or can one of the continental super-powers gain their revenge?

That story is still to be told, but for now revel in a vintage year with The Official ITV Sport Champions League Annual 2009. Enjoy the book.

itv SPORT

Moscow Magic – for United

English football was the pride of Europe as two Premier League sides contested the final of the Champions League for the first time on a famous night in May.

And Manchester United and Chelsea did the country proud in Moscow as the two great rivals served up a memorable match which went all the way to penalties.

In the most tension-packed finale possible it was United who finally held their nerve the best to win the shoot-out 6-5 and lift the trophy after 120 minutes of football had failed to separate the sides.

United went into the Moscow showpiece as domestic champions after holding off the late challenge of Chelsea to retain their Premier League crown.

And the way they started in the final suggested that a repeat of their famous 1999 double might be plain-sailing.

Portuguese star Cristiano Ronaldo headed United in front after 26 minutes when he connected with a cross from Wes Brown to score his 42nd-goal of a remarkable season.

Carlos Tevez and Michael Carrick almost doubled the lead but Chelsea keeper Petr Cech made outstanding saves.

And Chelsea hit back just before half-time when

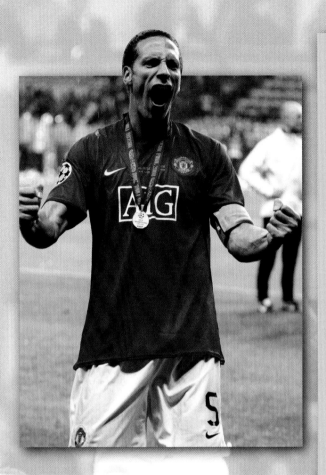

Frank Lampard made the most of a couple of kind deflections to lift a shot over Edwin van der Sar after the Dutch keeper slipped.

The Londoners then took control in the second half but could not force a winner as Didier Drogba's long-range curler hit a post.

Chelsea were also denied by the woodwork in injury-time as Lampard clipped a shot against the bar.

But United rallied late on and substitute Ryan Giggs had a header cleared off the line by John Terry before Drogba was sent off to set up the thrilling climax of the penalty shoot-out and United's night of Moscow magic.

Triumphant boss Alex Ferguson savoured the victory which gave the Scot – the most successful manager in British football history – the 18th major honour of his 22-year reign at Old Trafford.

He said: "We were fantastic in the first half but the goal gave them an impetus and they were the better team in the second half.

"But in extra-time I think we were the better team. It was tight and there were some fantastic moments. I feel very, very proud. It is a fantastic achievement."

Moscow Misery – for Chelsea

For every winner there has to be a loser and while Manchester United celebrated their Champions League triumph, for Chelsea it was a case of so near yet so far.

After losing three times at the semi-final stage, Chelsea made it through to the final by getting past old enemies Liverpool in the last four.

But victory in Moscow was cruelly denied them in a penalty shoot-out and within a week manager Avram Grant had lost his job.

The margin between success and failure could hardly have been smaller once Frank Lampard had cancelled out Cristiano Ronaldo's goal to leave Chelsea and Manchester United deadlocked at 1-1.

Chelsea were then just one kick away from glory but after captain John Terry hit the post with his spot-kick, Nicolas Anelka was denied by Edwin van der Sar and the trophy was on its way to Old Trafford, rather than Stamford Bridge for the first time.

"It's very hard to lose on penalties," said Grant, who lasted less than 12 months as José Mourinho's successor at Chelsea after seeing United also win the Premier League title race.

"Apart from the first 30 minutes we dominated the game. We hit the post and bar, but we lost. I'm very, very proud of the way we played. The spirit of the team was great and the quality was good."

Penalties – the Pleasure and Pain

Nine months after starting out on the road to Champions League glory, for Manchester United and Chelsea it all came down to penalty kicks.

After the final in Moscow ended deadlocked at 1-1, it took a shoot-out to separate the top teams in English football.

And after a heart-stopping chapter of twists and turns and tears of joy and sorrow, it was United who emerged victorious to again become Champions of Europe.

Here is how the drama unfolded:

Carlos Tevez went first for United and scored to make it 1-0.

German international Michael Ballack showed his usual coolness to make it 1-1.

Michael Carrick also held his nerve to restore United's advantage at 2-1.

Juliano Belletti, who had just come on, scored for Chelsea

with his only touch to level again at 2-2.

Cristiano Ronaldo had missed a spot-kick in the semis and did it again as Petr Cech's save left it at 2-2.

Frank Lampard again showed tremendous character to give Chelsea the advantage for the first time at 3-2.

Owen Hargreaves kept United in the hunt by converting to level it at 3-3.

Ashley Cole made sure that the momentum stayed with Chelsea, though, as he netted to make it 4-3.

Substitute Nani had to score for United and did so to keep the tie alive at 4-4.

Chelsea captain John Terry had one kick to win it but with his hands virtually on the trophy he slipped and sent his

effort against the post to leave the score at 4-4.

With United reprieved, Anderson, who had just come on, blasted home to give his side the lead again at 5-4.

Now sudden death, Salomon Kalou maintained the suspense by levelling it up again at 5-5.

Fittingly, record-breaker Ryan Giggs was next up for United and crucially scored to make it 6-5.

Nicolas Anelka had to score but Edwin van der Sar saved from the France international to become United's hero.

Nicolas Anelka sees his penalty saved by Edwin van der Sar

Penalties – Heroes and Villains

Manchester United goalkeeper Edwin van der Sar took on the mantle of hero for his team as he saved Nicolas Anelka's penalty to make United champions of Europe.

For the 37-year-old it meant a second European title following his previous success with Dutch club Ajax in 1995.

And United's success in Moscow also helped erase the memory of Ajax's final defeat 12 months later to Juventus, when the Dutch international finished on the wrong end of a penalty shoot-out.

"We didn't really want penalties but when the moment comes you know you can be a hero," van der Sar said.

"It's one of the benefits of having a long career. I won this final in 1995 with Ajax and I lost one on penalties so I know it's hard.

"When I lost the Champions League final in 1996 I was heartbroken and didn't leave the house for three days so it's good this has gone my way."

Sadly for Chelsea captain John Terry, he experienced the other side of the coin as his missed penalty cost his team the Champions League.

Terry had shown immense bravery to line up in the final after dislocating an elbow in Chelsea's final league match of the season less than a fortnight earlier.

His headed clearance off the line from Ryan Giggs in extra-time also kept the Londoners in with a chance of their first Champions League title.

But when a successful spot-kick in the shoot-out that followed would have given Chelsea glory, the luckless Terry slipped and hit the post.

The distraught England international was inconsolable afterwards, despite the efforts of his manager Avram Grant.

"He cried but he is the main reason we are here. He was there whenever we needed him as a captain. It happens unfortunately, but he is still a great captain and a great player," Grant said.

A dejected John Terry after Chelsea's defeat

Record-breaking Giggs Crowns Night of Glory

Champions League winners Manchester United could not have chosen a more fitting player to score their decisive penalty in the shoot-out which gave them the trophy than Ryan Giggs.

Giggs scored United's decisive sixth penalty on the night he also set a new record of appearances for the Old Trafford club.

When the 34-year-old winger came off the bench to replace Paul Scholes in the 87th-minute in Moscow he chalked up his 759th game for United.

Giggs, who made his league debut in 1991, passed the mark previously set by Sir Bobby Charlton, who was in the crowd and joined the United players in going up to receive their medals.

"It is a proud achievement for myself and my family but in the end it's all about winning trophies," said Giggs.

And he should know. The former Wales international has won 20 major honours in his days at United, including ten Premier League titles.

His latest came in the 2007/08 season and of course it was Giggs, one of British football's greatest players, who made sure United would finish top of the table by scoring their last-day winner at Wigan.

European Glory is Fitting Tribute to the Babes

Many people felt Manchester United were destined to win the Champions League in 2008 – and they were proved right.

Fifty years after the Munich air crash, in which eight of United's young players lost their lives, United paid tribute to the 'Busby Babes' in the best possible way by being crowned kings of Europe.

"We had a cause which was very important. People with causes are difficult to battle against and I think fate was playing its part," said manager Alex Ferguson.

Ferguson was following in the footsteps of Sir Matt Busby, who had been determined to establish United as the top team in Europe.

Busby, who became manager at Old Trafford in 1945, entered Manchester United into the

European Cup at a time when the English football authorities were not keen on the idea.

He had built a young side which had started to dominate English football by winning the league title in 1956 and 1957.

In their first attempt at the European Cup, United lost to holders Real Madrid in the semi-finals in 1957 and the following year disaster struck.

United had been playing a quarter-final second leg away to Red Star Belgrade when they stopped in Germany on the way home for their plane to re-fuel.

In bad weather on February 6, 1958, the plane crashed when

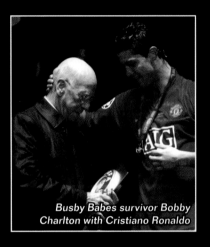

Busby Babes survivor Bobby Charlton with Cristiano Ronaldo

trying to take off and 23 people were killed, including United players Geoff Bent, Roger Byrne, Eddie Colman, Duncan Edwards, Mark Jones, David Pegg, Billy Whelan and Tommy Taylor.

Busby was near death himself but fought back to fitness and re-built the club to finally win the European Cup against Benfica at Wembley ten years later – building a legacy continued by Ferguson's current team.

How the Cup was Won...

Manchester United 1 (Ronaldo 26mins), Chelsea 1 (Lampard 45mins)

Manchester United won 6-5 on penalties

Attendance: 69,552

Referee: Lubos Michel (Slovakia).

MANCHESTER UNITED
Van der Sar
Brown (Anderson 120),
Ferdinand, Vidic, Evra
Hargreaves, Scholes (Giggs 87),
Carrick, Ronaldo
Rooney (Nani 101), Tevez

Substitutes not used:
Kuszczak, O'Shea, Fletcher, Silvestre.

Booked:
Scholes, Ferdinand, Vidic, Tevez.

CHELSEA
Cech
Essien, Carvalho, Terry, Ashley Cole
Ballack, Makelele (Belletti 120), Lampard
Joe Cole (Anelka 99), Malouda (Kalou 92)
Drogba

Substitutes not used:
Cudicini, Shevchenko, Obi, Alex.

Sent Off: Drogba (116).

Booked: Makelele, Carvalho, Ballack, Essien.

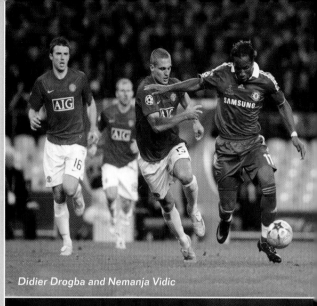

Didier Drogba and Nemanja Vidic

Joe Cole and Patrice Evra

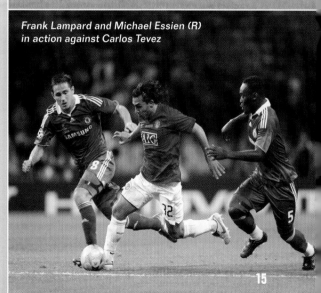

Frank Lampard and Michael Essien (R) in action against Carlos Tevez

The Road to Moscow

MATCHDAY 1 – TUESDAY 18 SEPTEMBER

Grp	Home		Away
A	Marseille	2-0	Besiktas
A	Porto	1-1	Liverpool
B	Chelsea	1-1	Rosenborg
B	Schalke	0-1	Valencia
C	Real Madrid	2-1	Bremen
C	Olympiacos	1-1	Lazio
D	AC Milan	2-1	Benfica
D	Shakhtar	2-0	Celtic

MATCHDAY 1 - WEDNESDAY 19 SEPTEMBER

Grp	Home		Away
E	Rangers	2-1	Stuttgart
E	Barcelona	3-0	Lyon
F	Roma	2-0	Dynamo Kyiv
F	Sporting Lisbon	0-1	Man. United
G	PSV	2-1	CSKA Moskva
G	Fenerbahçe	1-0	Inter Milan
H	Arsenal	3-0	Sevilla
H	Slavia	2-1	Steaua

MATCHDAY 2 – TUESDAY 2 OCTOBER

Grp	Home		Away
E	Lyon	0-3	Rangers
E	Stuttgart	0-2	Barcelona
F	Man. United	1-0	Roma
F	Dynamo Kyiv	1-2	Sporting Lisbon
G	Inter Milan	2-0	PSV
G	CSKA Moskva	2-2	Fenerbahçe
H	Steaua	0-1	Arsenal
H	Sevilla	4-2	Slavia

MATCHDAY 2 - WEDNESDAY 3 OCTOBER

Grp	Home		Away
A	Liverpool	0-1	Marseille
A	Besiktas	0-1	Porto
B	Valencia	1-2	Chelsea
B	Rosenborg	0-2	Schalke
C	Lazio	2-2	Real Madrid
C	Bremen	1-3	Olympiacos
D	Celtic	2-1	AC Milan
D	Benfica	0-1	Shakhtar

MATCHDAY 3 – TUESDAY 23 OCTOBER

Grp	Home		Away
E	Stuttgart	0-2	Lyon
E	Rangers	0-0	Barcelona
F	Dynamo Kyiv	2-4	Man. United
F	Roma	2-1	Sporting Lisbon
G	CSKA Moskva	1-2	Inter Milan
G	PSV	0-0	Fenerbahçe
H	Sevilla	2-1	Steaua
H	Arsenal	7-0	Slavia

MATCHDAY 3 - WEDNESDAY 24 OCTOBER

Grp	Home		Away
A	Besiktas	2-1	Liverpool
A	Marseille	1-1	Porto
B	Rosenborg	2-0	Valencia
B	Chelsea	2-0	Schalke
C	Bremen	2-1	Lazio
C	Real Madrid	4-2	Olympiacos
D	Benfica	1-0	Celtic
D	AC Milan	4-1	Shakhtar

FC Porto's Ricardo Quaresma

Group Results

MATCHDAY 4 – TUESDAY 6 NOVEMBER

Grp	Home		Away
A	Liverpool	8-0	Besiktas
A	Porto	2-1	Marseille
B	Valencia	0-2	Rosenborg
B	Schalke	0-0	Chelsea
C	Lazio	2-1	Bremen
C	Olympiacos	0-0	Real Madrid
D	Celtic	1-0	Benfica
D	Shakhtar	0-3	AC Milan

MATCHDAY 4 - WEDNESDAY 7 NOVEMBER

Grp	Home		Away
E	Lyon	4-2	Stuttgart
E	Barcelona	2-0	Rangers
F	Man. United	4-0	Dynamo Kyiv
F	Sporting Lisbon	2-2	Roma
G	Inter Milan	4-2	CSKA Moskva
G	Fenerbahçe	2-0	PSV
H	Steaua	0-2	Sevilla
H	Slavia	0-0	Arsenal

Liverpool's Peter Crouch scores against Besiktas

MATCHDAY 5 – TUESDAY 27 NOVEMBER

Grp	Home		Away
E	Stuttgart	3-2	Rangers
E	Lyon	2-2	Barcelona
F	Dynamo Kyiv	1-4	Roma
F	Man. United	2-1	Sporting Lisbon
G	CSKA Moskva	0-1	PSV
G	Inter Milan	3-0	Fenerbahçe
H	Sevilla	3-1	Arsenal
H	Steaua	1-1	Slavia

MATCHDAY 5 - WEDNESDAY 28 NOVEMBER

Grp	Home		Away
A	Besiktas	2-1	Marseille
A	Liverpool	4-1	Porto
B	Rosenborg	0-4	Chelsea
B	Valencia	0-0	Schalke
C	Bremen	3-2	Real Madrid
C	Lazio	1-2	Olympiacos
D	Benfica	1-1	AC Milan
D	Celtic	2-1	Shakhtar

MATCHDAY 6 – TUESDAY 4 DECEMBER

Grp	Home		Away
D	AC Milan	1-0	Celtic
D	Shakhtar	1-2	Benfica

MATCHDAY 6 - TUESDAY 11 DECEMBER

Grp	Home		Away
A	Marseille	0-4	Liverpool
A	Porto	2-0	Besiktas
B	Chelsea	0-0	Valencia
B	Schalke	3-1	Rosenborg
C	Real Madrid	3-1	Lazio
C	Olympiacos	3-0	Bremen

MATCHDAY 6 - WEDNESDAY 12 DECEMBER

Grp	Home		Away
E	Rangers	0-3	Lyon
E	Barcelona	3-1	Stuttgart
F	Roma	1-1	Man. United
F	Sporting Lisbon	3-0	Dynamo Kyiv
G	PSV	0-1	Inter Milan
G	Fenerbahçe	3-1	CSKA Moskva
H	Arsenal	2-1	Steaua
H	Slavia	0-3	Sevilla

The Road to Moscow

Group A	P	W	D	L	GD	Pts
FC Porto	6	3	2	1	1	11
Liverpool	6	3	1	2	13	10
Marseille	6	2	1	3	-3	7
Besiktas	6	2	0	4	-11	6

Group B	P	W	D	L	GD	Pts
Chelsea	6	3	3	0	7	12
FC Schalke 04	6	2	2	2	1	8
Rosenborg	6	2	1	3	-4	7
Valencia	6	1	2	3	-4	5

Group C	P	W	D	L	GD	Pts
Real Madrid	6	3	2	1	4	11
Olympiakos FC	6	3	2	1	4	11
Werder Bremen	6	2	0	4	-5	6
Lazio	6	1	2	3	-3	5

Group D	P	W	D	L	GD	Pts
AC Milan	6	4	1	1	7	13
Celtic	6	3	0	3	-1	9
Benfica	6	2	1	3	-1	7
Shakhtar Donetsk	6	2	0	4	-5	6

Celtic's Paul Hartley in action with AC Milan's Marek Jankulovski

Final Group Tables

Group E	P	W	D	L	GD	Pts
Barcelona	6	4	2	0	9	14
Olympique Lyonnais	6	3	1	2	1	10
Rangers	6	2	1	3	-2	7
VfB Stuttgart	6	1	0	5	-8	3

Group F	P	W	D	L	GD	Pts
Manchester United	6	5	1	0	9	16
Roma	6	3	2	1	5	11
Sporting Lisbon	6	2	1	3	1	7
Dynamo Kiev	6	0	0	6	-15	0

Group G	P	W	D	L	GD	Pts
Inter Milan	6	5	0	1	8	15
Fenerbahçe	6	3	2	1	2	11
PSV Eindhoven	6	2	1	3	-3	7
CSKA Moscow	6	0	1	5	-7	1

Group H	P	W	D	L	GD	Pts
Sevilla	6	5	0	1	7	15
Arsenal	6	4	1	1	10	13
Slavia Prague	6	1	2	3	-11	5
FC Steaua Bucharest	6	0	1	5	-6	1

FC Barcelona's Deco in action against Manchester United's Carlos Tevez

The Road to Moscow

Schalke 04 (p)	1	0	1(4)
Porto	0	1	1(1)

Schalke 04	0	0	0
Barcelona	1	1	2

Celtic	2	0	2
Barcelona	3	1	4

Roma	2	2	4
Real Madrid	1	1	2

Roma	0	0	0
Manchester United	2	1	3

Lyon	1	0	1
Manchester United	1	1	2

Arsenal	0	2	2
AC Milan	0	0	0

Arsenal	1	2	3
Liverpool	1	4	5

Liverpool	2	1	3
Inter Milan	0	0	0

Fenerbahçe (p)	3	2	5(3)
Sevilla	2	3	5(2)

Fenerbahçe	2	0	2
Chelsea	1	2	3

Olympiacos	0	0	0
Chelsea	0	3	3

Knock-out Stages

SEMI-FINALS

FINAL		
Manchester United (p)	1(6)
Chelsea	1(5)

Barcelona	0	0	**0**
Manchester United	0	1	**1**

Liverpool	1	2	**3**
Chelsea (aet)	1	3	**4**

Goal-den Boys – The Top Scorers

Cristiano Ronaldo's remarkable season for Manchester United saw him scoop nearly every individual award going.

And to add to his collection, the wing wizard finished as the top scorer in the Champions League.

Ronaldo scored eight times in the 2007/08 competition - to boost his overall tally for the campaign to a remarkable 42 - including United's goal against Chelsea in the final, to head a list of awesome goal-busting talent.

Ronaldo's nearest challengers not surprisingly came from English clubs, plus Barcelona – the only non Premier League side to reach the last four.

Chelsea hot-shot Didier Drogba could not add to his tally in the Moscow final so finished tied in second spot – two behind Ronaldo along with the Liverpool pair of Fernando Torres and Steven Gerrard and Barca star Lionel Messi.

Player	Goals	Club
Cristiano Ronaldo	8	Manchester United
Didier Drogba	6	Chelsea
Steven Gerrard	6	Liverpool
Fernando Torres	6	Liverpool
Lionel Messi	6	Barcelona
Raúl González	5	Real Madrid
Ryan Babel	5	Liverpool
Dirk Kuyt	5	Liverpool
Deivid	5	Fenerbahçe
Frédéric Kanouté	5	Sevilla
Zlatan Ibrahimovic	5	Inter Milan
Mirko Vu ini	4	Roma
Liedson	4	Sporting Lisbon
Wayne Rooney	4	Manchester United
Carlos Tévez	4	Manchester United
Cesc Fábregas	4	Arsenal
Luis Fabiano	4	Sevilla
Frank Lampard	4	Chelsea
Karim Benzema	4	Lyon
Filippo Inzaghi	4	AC Milan
Ruud van Nistelrooy	4	Real Madrid
Robinho	4	Real Madrid
Goran Pandev	4	Lazio

FC Barcelona's Thierry Henry

Scholes and Giggs Join the 100 Club

Manchester United's midfield maestro Paul Scholes joined a select band when he made his 100th appearance in the Champions League in United's semi-final first leg in Barcelona.

Scholes, who made his Champions League debut in 1994, is the latest of just nine players to have reached the century mark.

Team-mate Ryan Giggs joined the exclusive club earlier in the 2007/08 campaign to take his place alongside former Old Trafford team-mate David Beckham, while United club captain Gary Neville is just one game short.

The list is headed by Real Madrid's legendary Spanish striker Raul, who is also the competition's leading goalscorer.

Scholes enjoyed a memorable Champions League campaign as he finally made up for missing United's 1999 final triumph against Bayern Munich through suspension by helping his team to overcome Chelsea and lift the trophy for a second time.

Ferguson said: "The disappointment of '99 has gone now for him. I'm delighted for the boy. He is a fantastic person," said United manager Alex Ferguson, who honoured his long-standing promise to give Scholes a place in his final team.

"People like Scholes, Giggs and Neville: they know what Manchester United means."

Paul Scholes joined the Champions League century club on Wednesday when he made his 100th appearance in the competition for Manchester United in the semi-final, first leg against Barcelona at the Nou Camp.

His century, which does not include matches in the qualifying round, comes 14 years after his first appearance also against Barcelona, in a 2-2 draw at Old Trafford in October 1994.

Scholes, 33, becomes only the ninth player to make 100 appearances in the competition proper, according to official figures issued by UEFA, European soccer's governing body.

He has scored 20 goals.

Scholes's United midfield partner Ryan Giggs made his 100th Champions League appearance against Olympique Lyon last month and made his 102nd appearance when he came on as a substitute against Barca. United club captain Gary Neville has made 99 appearances for United in the competition proper.

The other seven players to make 100 appearances in the competition are Raul (116), Roberto Carlos (114), Paolo Maldini (109), Oliver Kahn (103), David Beckham (103), Clarence Seedorf (101) and Luis Figo (100). Maldini holds the record for all European club competitions with 172 appearances.

Champions League appearances (group stage to final only)

- 116 Raúl González (Real Madrid)
- 114 Roberto Carlos (Real Madrid, Fenerbahçe)
- 109 Paolo Maldini (AC Milan)
- 103 David Beckham (Manchester United, Real Madrid)
- 103 Oliver Kahn (Bayern Munich)
- 103 Ryan Giggs (Manchester United)
- 101 Paul Scholes (Manchester United)
- 101 Clarence Seedorf (Ajax, Real Madrid, AC Milan)
- 100 Luís Figo (Barcelona, Real Madrid, Inter Milan)

Champions League goals

- 61 Raúl González (Real Madrid)
- 53 Ruud van Nistelrooy (PSV Eindhoven, Manchester United, Real Madrid)
- 47 Andriy Shevchenko (Dynamo Kyiv, AC Milan, Chelsea)
- 45 Thierry Henry (AS Monaco, Arsenal, Barcelona)
- 42 Filippo Inzaghi (Juventus, AC Milan)
- 37 Alessandro Del Piero (Juventus)

Celtic – Pride of Scotland

Scottish champions Celtic enjoyed another memorable Champions League campaign as they qualified for the knock-out phase for the second year running, having never previously made it through the group stages.

Unfortunately for Gordon Strachan's men, Barcelona blocked their route to the quarter-finals as they completed a 4-2 aggregate victory.

But the Celtic fans still had plenty of nights to celebrate in Glasgow as they went through from Group D with a 100 per cent record at Celtic Park.

First, though, the Hoops had to negotiate a dramatic qualifying tie against Russian side Spartak Moscow, which went all the way to penalties.

With the aggregate score locked at 2-2, Celtic triumphed in the shoot-out at Celtic Park with goalkeeper Artur Boruc emerging as the hero as he saved two attempts from Spartak to take Celtic through 4-3.

Strachan's side then found itself in a group

alongside Shakhtar Donetsk, Benfica and Italian giants AC Milan.

Never the best of travellers, Celtic opened with a 2-0 defeat in Ukraine to Shakhtar but a thrilling 2-1 home win over AC Milan got their campaign up and running.

Stephen McManus put the Scots ahead and then after Kaka had equalised from the penalty spot, Scott McDonald pounced with a last-minute winner to give Celtic one of their most famous wins.

Celtic then faced two crucial games against Benfica as the battle for the second qualifying spot hotted up. They lost the first 1-0 in Portugal but turned the tables by reversing the scoreline in Glasgow with Aiden McGeady getting the all-important goal on the stroke of half-time.

Jan Vennegoor of Hesselink celebrates scoring the first goal for Celtic at Celtic Park against FC Barcelona in the second round of the Champions League

Celtic celebrate after Stephen McManus scores their first goal against AC Milan in the group stages of the tournament at Celtic Park

The Hoops then needed to beat Shakhtar at home and again, thanks to another nerve-wracking finish, they managed it. With the scores level at 1-1 and time running out, Massimo Donati struck with a deflected shot to lift Celtic into second place behind group winners AC Milan.

And despite a 1-0 defeat in Milan in their final group game, Shakhtar's loss at home to Benfica was enough to take Celtic through and spark a night of celebration for the hordes of visiting fans in the San Siro Stadium.

Celtic were then handed a glamour tie against Barcelona in the last-16 but the Catalans, the last team to win at Celtic in a Champions League tie four years previously, turned on the style at Celtic Park to take a grip of the tie.

Celtic led twice through headers from Jan Vennegoor of Hesselink and Barry Robson but Barcelona then dominated the second half and after Thierry Henry had equalised with a stunning strike, Lionel Messi's second goal of the game 11 minutes from time gave Barca a 3-2 win.

Faced with a mountain to climb in the Nou Camp, an early goal scuppered Celtic's slender hopes of a quarter-final place, but again they could look back on their European adventure with great pride.

Champions League Quiz

1. Who finished as top scorer in the 2007/08 Champions League?

2. Which was the only non-English team to make it to the semi-finals of the 2007/08 Champions League?

3. Which two clubs share the record number of three wins each since the Champions League was introduced in 1992/93?

4. Whose penalty did Edwin van der Sar save to win the 2007/08 Champions League final for Manchester United?

5. Who scored Chelsea's equaliser in the 2007/08 final in Moscow?

6. Who is the only player to have won the Champions League with three different clubs?

7. Liverpool set a new goal-scoring record when they won a group match 8-0 in the 2007/08 competition. Who did they beat?

8. Who has made the most appearances and scored the most goals in the Champions League?

9. Which country does Barcelona star Lionel Messi play for?

10. Who was sent off in the final of the 2007/08 Champions League?

11. Which former Bury, Brighton and Sheffield United striker scored against Chelsea for Fenerbahçe in the 2007/08 Champions League quarter-finals?

12. Which Scottish club went out of the Champions League at the group stage but went on to reach the final of the 2007/08 Uefa Cup?

Answers on page 61

Liverpool's Steven Gerrard

Not This Time for Rafa's Reds – The Liverpool Story

Only Real Madrid and AC Milan have managed more than Liverpool's five successes in Europe's premier cup competition.

After four wins in the European Cup, Liverpool added the Champions League to their collection in 2005.

They again reached the final in 2007 but in 2008 their hopes of further glory were dashed at the semi-final stage as Chelsea finally gained their revenge on their Premier League rivals.

After beating the Londoners in the last four in 2005 and 2007, Liverpool could not make it a hat-trick to reach the final in Moscow but having almost crashed out in the group stages the Reds, who finished only fourth in the domestic league, had once again saved their best for Europe.

Rafael Benitez's side cruised through their qualifying tie against Toulouse but immediately ran into trouble in Group A when they followed up a 1-1 draw at Porto by suffering a shock 1-0 home defeat to Marseille.

Things got even worse for the Reds when they then slumped to a 2-1 loss at Besiktas when a late goal from Steven Gerrard could not prevent them from a result which left them needing maximum points from their last three games, and other results to go their way, to progress.

Thankfully for the Merseysiders they finally clicked into gear in the return meeting against Besiktas when they hit the hapless Turks with a competition record 8-0 win. Midfielder Yossi Benayoun led the goal glut with a hat-trick with the other goals coming from Peter Crouch (2), Ryan Babel (2) and Gerrard.

Inter Milan v Liverpool at the San Siro Stadium in the second round of the competition

Fernando Torres scores against Arsenal in the quarter final second leg at Anfield

Porto were then despatched 4-1 thanks to two goals from Fernando Torres to set up a make-or-break clash against Marseille in France to decide second place behind Porto.

And the Reds rose to the challenge magnificently, romping to a 4-0 win with Torres, Babel, Dirk Kuyt and Gerrard – who became the club's record goalscorer in Europe – all on target.

Gerrard and Kuyt hit the net again as Inter Milan were beaten 2-0 at Anfield in the last-16 first leg and Liverpool completed the job with a 1-0 win in San Siro thanks to Torres to set up a quarter-final clash with great rivals Arsenal.

The first leg at the Emirates Stadium ended all square at 1-1 thanks to an equaliser by Kuyt to set up a classic return leg at Anfield.

Arsenal led through Abou Diaby and then after Sami Hyypia and Torres - with a brilliant goal - had scored, it looked as though they would go through on away goals thanks to Emmanuel Adebayor's 84th-minute equaliser to make it 2-2.

But in a pulsating finish Liverpool went straight to the other end and grabbed the lead through a Gerrard penalty before Babel finally made sure of a famous 4-2 victory by scoring in injury-time.

Once again then Liverpool and Chelsea met in the semi-finals but this time there would be no happy ending for the Reds.

A late John Arne Riise own-goal to cancel out Kuyt's effort in the first leg at Anfield handed Chelsea the advantage but with Didier Drogba and Torres both scoring at Stamford Bridge the stalemate went into extra-time.

Finally, though, Chelsea took control with a Frank Lampard penalty and another for Drogba proving too much for even Babel's late screamer to overcome as Liverpool's dream of another title was ended.

Still Waiting for Euro Glory – The Arsenal Story

The Champions League crown remains tantalisingly out of reach for Arsenal and long-serving manager Arsene Wenger and the 2007/08 campaign again brought them no nearer to their elusive goal.

The Gunners have won three Premier League titles and four FA Cups under the mercurial Frenchman and reached the final of the Champions League in 2006.

But since then they have come up short with their latest attempt ending at the quarter-final stage to domestic rivals Liverpool.

Arsenal breezed through their qualifying-round tie against Sparta Prague, winning 5-0 on aggregate to earn their place in a not-too-demanding Group H alongside Sevilla, Slavia Prague and Steaua Bucharest.

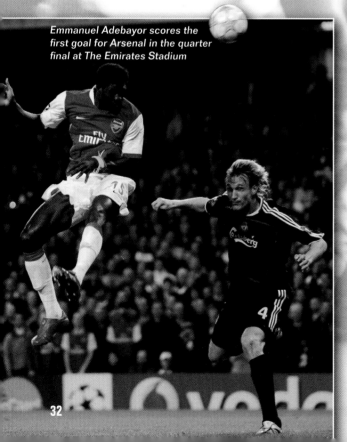

Emmanuel Adebayor scores the first goal for Arsenal in the quarter final at The Emirates Stadium

And Wenger's men could not have made a better start as they beat a Sevilla side managed by future Tottenham boss Juande Ramos 3-0 at the Emirates Stadium thanks to goals from Cesc Fabregas, Robin van Persie and Eduardo.

Van Persie struck again as Steaua Bucharest were beaten 1-0 in Romania and Arsenal then hit top form by equalling their best ever win in the competition with a 7-0 destruction of Slavia Prague.

Theo Walcott came of age as a Gunner as the teenager netted twice, with Fabregas (two), Alex Hleb, Nicklas Bendtner and an own-goal completing the rout as the in-form Gunners recorded a 12th straight victory at home and abroad.

That momentum wasn't maintained but a 0-0 draw in Prague was enough to take Arsenal through to the last-16 of the Champions League with two games to spare.

Unfortunately for the Londoners they were unable to top the group as a 3-1 defeat in Spain to Sevilla ended a 28-match unbeaten run but at least Arsenal signed off with a win by beating Steaua 2-0 with goals from Diaby and Bendtner.

That earned the Gunners a last-16 tie with holders and 3-times winners AC Milan and the two-legged tie clash against the Italians brought Arsenal one of their best ever results in Europe.

After the first leg ended 0-0 at the Emirates, AC Milan were overwhelming favourites to reach the quarter-finals but Arsenal produced a memorable performance in the San Siro Stadium to win 2-0.

AC Milan v Arsenal in the second round of the competition at The San Siro Stadium

Late goals from Fabregas and Emmanuel Adebayor saw Arsenal become the first English club to win at Milan and earned them a last-eight date with Liverpool.

But sadly for Arsenal that proved to be the end of the road as they bowed out in heart-breaking fashion at Anfield.

Despite another goal from Adebayor, the Gunners were held 1-1 in the home leg and looked up against it going up to Liverpool.

But after dominating and leading through Abou Diaby's first-half goal they fought back from 2-1 down to score again through Adebayor following a piece of brilliance from Walcott to nose ahead on away goals.

Arsenal were just six minutes away from reaching the semi-finals but their hopes were dashed when Steven Gerrard restored Liverpool's lead from a disputed penalty and Ryan Babel clinched a 4-2 win in stoppage-time to leave Wenger still waiting for the ultimate prize.

Champions League Legends

RAUL GONZALEZ

Club: Real Madrid

Position: Striker

Country: Spain

Date of birth: 27/06/77

Champions League appearances 2007/08: 8

Goals: 5

The Spanish legend is the only player to have scored in two Champions League finals, scoring for Real Madrid in their 2000 and 2002 triumphs.

Those goals and five more in the 2007/08 campaign have helped Raul become the highest goalscorer in Champions League history with 64 goals.

He also holds the record for most appearances in the competition with 116 thanks to a remarkable 14-year first-team career with Real Madrid – his only senior club.

Raul, who has been capped over 100 times by Spain, became the youngest player to make his senior Real debut when he first played at the age of 17.

He has since scored over 200 goals in La Liga and played his part in bringing six league titles and three Champions League trophies to the Bernabeu Stadium.

PAOLO MALDINI

Club: AC Milan

Position: Defender

Country: Italy

Date of birth: 26/06/68

Champions League appearances 2007/08: 4

Goals: 0

The seemingly ageless Italian defender has won a remarkable tally of five European Cups and Champions League titles with AC Milan.

His first came in 1989 as he formed a key part of the Milan 'Dream Team' that dominated Italian and European football for the next few years. From 1988 to 1996, Maldini shared in five Serie A titles and three European successes.

Maldini's most recent Champions League win came in 2007 and in all he has seven domestic championship medals in his collection.

A magnificent athlete and cultured left-sided defender, Maldini has played more Serie A games than any other player and has played in over 1,000 matches for club and country.

He holds the record for international caps with 126 and despite turning 40 in 2008 changed his mind about retiring after agreeing a new one-year contract at Milan to play on until the end of the 2008/09 season.

No Way José

The Champions League was the only trophy that eluded José Mourinho during his spectacular reign as Chelsea manager and he lasted only one match of a remarkable 2007/08 campaign which almost saw the Blues capture the European crown.

Six trophies in three years and an unbeaten home league record made Mourinho Chelsea's most successful ever manager.

But two semi-final appearances in the Champions League - both against Liverpool - were the nearest he came to emulating his 2004 success with Porto.

Relations between the 'Special One' and the Chelsea hierarchy were already seemingly strained when Chelsea were surprisingly held to a 1-1 home draw by Norwegian minnows Rosenborg in their opening game in Group B in September 2007 and Mourinho was soon on his way.

Director of football Avram Grant was his surprise successor and while no-one tipped him to be in the job for long, the Israeli ended up being only the width of a post away from delivering the Champions League title to Stamford Bridge.

Frank Lampard scores against Liverpool in the semi final at Stamford Bridge

Grant's first European test was passed with a 2-1 win in Valencia, despite a goal from home favourite David Villa as Joe Cole and Didier Drogba countered for the Blues.

A first home win for the new boss followed against Schalke thanks to goals from Florent Malouda and Drogba before the return trip to Germany ended in a 0-0 draw which

meant a victory in Rosenborg would take Chelsea into the knock-out phase.

And they didn't disappoint with a 4-0 win making amends for their opening result as Alex, Joe Cole and Drogba, with another two, found the back of the Norwegians' net before a goalless draw at home to Valencia completed an unbeaten qualification campaign.

Chelsea were drawn against Greek champions Olympiacos in the last-16 and following another 0-0 stalemate in Athens booked their quarter-final place thanks to a 3-0 win at the Bridge secured by goals from Michael Ballack, Frank Lampard and Salomon Kalou.

Grant's men appeared to have the luck of the draw when

they were then paired with Fenerbahçe, although a 2-1 defeat in Turkey left them with work to do in the home leg.

Injuries to Petr Cech and then Carlo Cudicini saw Hilario take over in goal and after an early header from Ballack gave Chelsea the advantage on away goals, Lampard finally settled the nerves with a late second to take the Blues into a fourth Champions League semi final in five years.

Again Liverpool blocked the path to the final but this time Chelsea emerged victorious. A 1-1 draw at Anfield, sealed by a late own-goal from Liverpool defender John Arne Riise, left the tie perfectly balanced but on a triumphant night at Stamford Bridge, Chelsea emerged victorious.

Drogba's 17th European goal, breaking the club record jointly held by Blues legend Peter Osgood, gave Chelsea the

lead but when Fernando Torres levelled, the game went into extra-time.

Fortunately for Chelsea they found a hero in Lampard who, back in the team following the death of his mother Pat, calmly restored the lead from

the penalty spot and then after Drogba had scored again, not even a late strike from Ryan Babel could prevent Grant's side from marching onto Moscow to meet Manchester United in the final.

The rest, as they, say is history.

Lionel Messi

CLUB:	**BARCELONA**
POSITION:	**FORWARD**
COUNTRY:	**ARGENTINA**
DATE OF BIRTH:	24/06/87
CHAMPIONS LEAGUE APPEARANCES 2007/08:	9
GOALS:	6

The young Argentinian has made such a big impact at Barcelona that he is vying with Manchester United's Cristiano Ronaldo for the unofficial title of the best player in the world.

When the pair met at Old Trafford in the 2007/08 Champions League semi-finals it was Messi who shone the brightest and his six goals in the competition left him just two behind Ronaldo as the leading scorer.

Injury problems have dogged Messi's early years at the Nou Camp but he has already played over 100 games for Barca and scored some spectacular individual goals to help them to two league titles and the 2005/06 Champions League.

A fantastic player with the ball at his feet, Messi's dribbling skills are a nightmare for defenders at club and international level where he has established himself as a key member of the Argentina team after being named as the Young Player of the Year in 2006 and 2007.

Fernando Torres

CLUB:	LIVERPOOL
POSITION:	STRIKER
COUNTRY:	SPAIN
DATE OF BIRTH:	20/03/84
CHAMPIONS LEAGUE APPEARANCES 2007/08:	10
GOALS:	6

The Spanish striker enjoyed a stunning first season at Liverpool following his arrival from Atletico Madrid in a £20-million deal, scoring 33 goals.

Twenty four of those came in the Premier League and six in the Champions League as Torres helped Liverpool reach the semi-finals, where they lost to Chelsea despite another goal from 'El Nino'.

At Anfield, Torres struck up a superb understanding with Steven Gerrard and his goal tally in the Premier League made him the highest scoring foreign player in his first season in English football.

A superb finisher who also leads the attack for Spain, Torres could be the key to Liverpool's hopes of ending their near 20-year wait to win a 19th English championship.

Classic Clashes
Champions League Highlights 2007/08

The dramatic climax to the 2007/08 Champions League final could not be beaten for drama as Manchester United overcame Chelsea on penalties to lift the trophy. But there were plenty of gripping moments en route to Moscow and here are a few of the highlights from earlier in the competition.

LIVERPOOL 4, ARSENAL 2 (5-3 ON AGGREGATE)

The quarter-final second leg between Liverpool and Arsenal was a classic as both teams had victory seemingly snatched from their grasp before Liverpool finally went through.

Sami Hyypia and Fernando Torres had put Liverpool ahead at Anfield but when Emmanuel Adebayor equalised late on to make the aggregate score 3-3 the Gunners had one foot in the semi-final thanks to the away-goals rule.

But immediately Liverpool went up the other end and when Kolo Toure was penalised for a foul on Ryan Babel, Steven Gerrard scored from the spot.

Even then a last-gasp goal from Arsenal would have taken them through but Babel finally broke their hearts with another goal in injury-time.

Sevilla 3, Fenerbahçe 2 (5-5 on aggregate, Fenerbahçe won 3-2 on penalties)

Turkish club Fenerbahçe reached the quarter-finals for the first time ever thanks to a remarkable result in Spain.

After winning the first leg 3-2, Fenerbahçe were 3-1 down by half-time in the return and facing the prospect of going out.

But Brazilian striker Deivid scored his second of the game to take the tie to extra-time and when no further goals were added it went to penalties.

Goalkeeper Volkan Demirel, who had been at fault for a couple of the earlier goals, then emerged as the Fenerbahçe hero as he saved three spot kicks to send Sevilla crashing out.

Liverpool 8, Besiktas 0

Liverpool deserved another mention for setting a competition record in their demolition of Turkish club Besiktas in the group stages.

The Reds were struggling to qualify at the time and had even lost away to Besiktas a couple of weeks earlier.

But in manager Rafa Benitez's 50th European match in charge they more than made amends, led to their rout by a hat-trick from midfielder Yossi Benayoun.

Werder Bremen 1, Olympiacos 3

Greek side Olympiacos had never won away from home in 31 previous attempts in the Champions League but finally hit the jackpot in Germany to help them qualify from Group C.

Werder Bremen took the lead but three goals in the final 20 minutes gave Olympiacos one of their best ever nights in Europe.

Ieroklis Stoltidis, Christos Patsatzoglou and Darko Kovacevic were the goal-scoring heroes for the Greeks.

REAL MADRID 1, ROMA 2 (2-4 ON AGGREGATE)

Three-times Champions League winners Real Madrid must have fancied their chances of securing yet another quarter-final place, despite a 2-1 defeat at AS Roma in the first leg of their first knock-out round tie.

But the Italians stood firm in the Bernabeu Stadium and after Pepe was sent off for Real, Roma increased their lead thanks to a superb Rodrigo Taddei header.

Raul pulled a goal back but Mirko Vucinic struck in the last minute to send Real out and give the 'Giallorossi' one of their best ever results in Europe.

Classic Clashes

CELTIC 2, BARCELONA 3

Scottish champions Celtic had enjoyed some outstanding results at Celtic Park in an unbeaten four-year run, including a terrific win over AC Milan in the group stages of the 2007/08 competition.

But the Hoops found the brilliance of Barcelona too hot to handle in the opening leg of their last-16 tie.

Celtic went ahead through Jan Vennegoor of Hesselink's thumping header and even though Lionel Messi levelled with a deflected shot the Scots led at half-time when Barry Robson headed home on his debut.

But with Barca committed to all-out attack with Messi, Ronaldinho and Thierry Henry playing up front they turned on the style in the second half.

Henry equalised when he curled in a shot reminiscent of his days with Arsenal and a feast of football was capped when Messi showed his class with another stunning finish to send the Catalans on their way towards the quarter-finals.

FENERBAHÇE 2, CHELSEA 1

Eventual finalists Chelsea had to come from behind in their quarter-final clash with Fenerbahçe after losing the first leg in Turkey to two spectacular goals.

And one of those will never be forgotten by the 'Coca Cola Kid' Colin Kazim-Richards, who came off the bench to score with a screamer.

Kazim-Richards, who got his nickname when Brighton fans won a competition run by the drinks' company to raise funds for his transfer fee from Bury, rocked Chelsea with his first goal in the Champions League.

Fenerbahçe had trailed to an early own-goal from Deivid and were second best until Kazim-Richards, who also had a spell with Sheffield United, took the game to Chelsea, who then conceded a second when Brazilian Deivid crashed in a shot from 35 yards.

Barcelona's Lionel Messi scores his side's first goal at Celtic Park

AC MILAN 0, ARSENAL 2 (0-2 ON AGGREGATE)

Italian giants AC Milan had never lost a Champions League game at home to an English club so Arsenal's prospects of reaching the quarter-finals looked bleak when they could only draw 0-0 in the first leg at the Emirates Stadium.

But one of the Gunners' finest ever performances in Europe ended that record as the holders were sent tumbling out by two late goals.

AC Milan dominated the opening stages but when Cesc Fabregas hit the bar late in the first half the tide was beginning to turn.

Some typically slick Arsenal football then had an ageing Milan side at full stretch and with five minutes to go Fabregas broke the deadlock with a fantastic goal as he ran at the Italians' defence before blasting home a shot from 25 yards.

Arsenal then completed victory in the final minute when Emmanuel Adebayor scored his first European goal for the club.

PORTO 1, SCHALKE 0 (1-1 ON AGGREGATE, SCHALKE WON 4-1 ON PENALTIES)

German club Schalke had never reached the quarter-finals of the Champions League until they held their nerve to beat 2004 Champions Porto on penalties.

Schalke had led 1-0 from the first leg but were pegged back late on in the return in Portugal when Lisandro Lopez equalised.

No goals in extra-time meant penalties when goalkeeper Manuel Neuer emerged as the shoot-out hero.

Neuer saved from Bruno Alves and Lopez which left Jermaine Jones to convert the clinching spot-kick and send Schalke through to meet Barcelona.

Cesc Fabregas celebrates his goal for 0-1 at The San Siro

PLAYER PROFILE

Zlatan Ibrahimovic

CLUB:	INTER MILAN
POSITION:	STRIKER
COUNTRY:	SWEDEN
DATE OF BIRTH:	03/10/81
CHAMPIONS LEAGUE APPEARANCES 2007/08:	7
GOALS:	5

The powerful Inter forward underlined his credentials as one of the top strikers in Europe with five goals in just seven Champions League appearances during the 2007/08 campaign.

That could not help the Milan club progress beyond the last-16 following their defeat to Liverpool but there has been no questioning their recent domination of Italian football.

Inter won their third straight Scudetto in 2008 with Ibrahimovic helping secure two of those titles following his arrival from Serie A rivals Juventus in 2006, where he also shared in two championship successes.

However, those honours were revoked following a match-rigging scandal in Italian footall which led to Juventus's relegation and a move for Swedish international Ibrahimovic, who started his career with a prolific spell at Ajax.

Ruud van Nistelrooy

CLUB:	**REAL MADRID**
POSITION:	**STRIKER**
COUNTRY:	**HOLLAND**
DATE OF BIRTH:	**01/07/76**
CHAMPIONS LEAGUE APPEARANCES 2007/08:	**7**
GOALS:	**4**

Four goals during the 2007/08 Champions League took Ruud van Nistelrooy past the 50-mark in the competition, placing him behind only Raul in the list of all-time scorers since the current format was introduced in 1992.

The Holland international has shared the goals between PSV Eindhoven, Manchester United and current club Real Madrid.

Van Nistelrooy scored a phenomenal 150 goals in five seasons at Old Trafford with 38 coming in the Champions League, making him United's top scorer in Europe.

In England he won every domestic honour and the goals have continued to flow with Real, where he has twice won La Liga and finished as the league's leading scorer in 2006/07.

Bojan Krkic

CLUB:	**BARCELONA**
POSITION:	**FORWARD**
COUNTRY:	**SPAIN**
DATE OF BIRTH:	**28/08/90**
CHAMPIONS LEAGUE APPEARANCES 2007/08:	**9**
GOALS:	**1**

Like Barcelona team-mate Lionel Messi, Bojan Krkic is another exciting prospect to emerge from the youth system at the Nou Camp.

The teenager scored a record-breaking 500 goals in youth football for Barca to earn promotion to the senior team almost as soon as he became a professional on his 17th-birthday.

A prodigious talent as a quick-footed attacking player, Krkic became the youngest player ever to score for Barcelona and with ten goals in La Liga during the 2007/08 season he broke Raul's club record for a debut season.

Often used as a substitute during Barca's run to the Champions League semi-finals in 2008, the Spain under-21 international looks to have a huge future ahead of him.

Cesc Fabregas

CLUB:	ARSENAL
POSITION:	MIDFIELDER
COUNTRY:	SPAIN
DATE OF BIRTH:	04/05/87
CHAMPIONS LEAGUE APPEARANCES 2007/08:	8
GOALS:	4

Despite his relative youth, the Arsenal midfielder is already one of the most important players in Arsene Wenger's side and is crucial to their hopes of getting back among the honours.

Wenger brought Fabregas to the Emirates Stadium from Barcelona before he had played a senior game but made him the Gunners' youngest ever first-team player when he gave him his debut at the age of 16.

Since then, the Spanish international has made almost 200 appearances for the London club, scoring 26 times including one of the goals in Arsenal's famous Champions League win at AC Milan in 2008.

However, it is his vision and range of passing that are his major qualities and it was no surprise that he was named as the PFA's young player of the year for 2007/08.

Karim Benzema

CLUB:	LYON
POSITION:	FORWARD
COUNTRY:	FRANCE
DATE OF BIRTH:	19/12/87
CHAMPIONS LEAGUE APPEARANCES 2007/08:	7
GOALS:	4

One of the brightest prospects in French football, along with team-mate Hatem Ben Arfar, the Lyon forward was linked with a move to Manchester United after scoring against the eventual champions in their last-16 tie of the Champions League in 2007/08.

However, Benzema pledged his future to Lyon by agreeing a new long-term contract to stay with the French League champions until 2013.

The France international and player-of-the-year has played his part in helping Lyon win their last four league titles.

A consistent scorer at club level, Benzema also made an impressive start to his international career and will be one to watch in future Champions League campaigns.

Cristiano Ronaldo

CLUB:	**MANCHESTER UNITED**
POSITION:	**FORWARD**
COUNTRY:	**PORTUGAL**
DATE OF BIRTH:	**05/02/85**
CHAMPIONS LEAGUE APPEARANCES 2007/08:	**11**
GOALS:	**8**

One of the world's best players, the Manchester United winger enjoyed a golden year in 2007/08.

The Portuguese international scored a remarkable 42 goals to help United win the Premier League and Champions League double – sparking renewed speculation that Real Madrid would try and lure him to the Bernabeu Stadium.

One of his eight goals in Europe came in the final and even though he missed a penalty in the shoot-out against Chelsea, the former Porto player still finished on the winning side.

Also used as a central striker by United manager Alex Ferguson, Ronaldo, as powerful in the air as he is at taking set pieces and when running with the ball, scored almost 100 goals in his first five years at Old Trafford.

Champions League Wordsearch

Can you find the 14 hidden words in the grid below?
The words can be vertical, horizontal, backwards or diagonal...

R	C	R	P	X	L	N	R	S	C	Z	Y	R
V	T	L	N	Y	Y	G	T	N	Z	S	V	C
Y	R	R	E	T	C	C	N	O	Z	E	G	Q
K	R	C	M	P	H	R	A	I	Z	I	N	G
W	G	N	E	E	H	W	L	P	X	T	W	L
Z	K	I	L	L	O	Q	I	M	K	L	C	I
N	G	S	G	C	T	T	M	A	N	A	R	V
F	E	K	S	G	H	I	B	H	P	N	O	E
A	Z	O	A	L	S	C	C	C	F	E	N	R
B	M	M	J	J	B	Z	E	Z	L	P	A	P
W	O	X	P	V	R	T	B	C	T	L	L	O
R	Y	B	A	R	C	E	L	O	N	A	D	O
F	E	R	G	U	S	O	N	Z	M	N	O	L

Champions   **Ronaldo**   **Milan**   **Liverpool**

Moscow   **Chelsea**   **Barcelona**   **Celtic**

Ferguson   **Terry**   **Penalties**

Giggs   **Cech**   **Roma**   *Answers on page 61*

FC Barcelona's Ronaldinho

David Villa

CLUB:	VALENCIA
POSITION:	STRIKER
COUNTRY:	SPAIN
DATE OF BIRTH:	03/12/81
CHAMPIONS LEAGUE APPEARANCES 2007/08:	5
GOALS:	2

Striker David Villa scored just twice in the 2007/08 Champions League as Valencia went out at the group stage but he can still claim to be one of the top strikers in Europe.

He underlined that point with Spain during Euro 2008 when he extended his impressive scoring streak in international football to raise his market value in the face of speculation linking him with moves to Real Madrid or the English Premier League.

A prolific scorer in Spanish club football, Villa started his career with Sporting Gijon before being elevated to La Liga with Real Zaragoza and then Valencia.

He has helped both Zaragoza and Valencia win the Spanish Cup and further honours surely beckon when he joins one of Europe's heavyweight clubs.

Francesco Totti

CLUB:	**AS ROMA**
POSITION:	**STRIKER**
COUNTRY:	**ITALY**
DATE OF BIRTH:	**27/09/76**
CHAMPIONS LEAGUE APPEARANCES 2007/08:	**6**
GOALS:	**1**

World Cup winner Francesco Totti missed Roma's quarter-final tie against Manchester United in the 2007/08 Champions League through injury and the Italians could not win without him.

But Totti has brought plenty of previous success to Roma, where he is a true legend after spending his entire career to date with the club.

The Rome-born striker has played over 500 games for his home city team and with over 200 goals is Roma's highest ever scorer.

Five times Italian footballer of the year, Totti has helped Roma win one Serie A title, as well as finishing runners-up five times, and five Italian cups, while he was also part of the Italy team that won the 2006 World Cup.

Pato

CLUB:	AC MILAN
POSITION:	FORWARD
COUNTRY:	BRAZIL
DATE OF BIRTH:	02/09/89
CHAMPIONS LEAGUE APPEARANCES 2007/08:	2
GOALS:	0

Teenager Pato made a minimal impact in the 2007/08 Champions League campaign but looks certain to be a huge star of the future at club and international level, having already made his full debut for Brazil.

Pato started his career with Brazilian club Internacional, helping them win the FIFA Club World Cup in 2006, when he took Pele's record as the youngest ever goalscorer in a FIFA competition.

AC Milan then won the race to sign the talented young striker in August, 2007 and gave him his senior debut as soon as permitted the following January.

Pato scored on his Serie A debut and with nine goals in his first 20 appearances for Milan there are sure to be plenty more to come.

Frederic Kanoute

CLUB:	SEVILLA
POSITION:	FORWARD
COUNTRY:	MALI
DATE OF BIRTH:	02/09/77
CHAMPIONS LEAGUE APPEARANCES 2007/08:	8
GOALS:	5

Striker 'Fredi' Kanoute had a mixed time while playing in England but has been a big hit with Spanish club Sevilla.

The Mali international played for both West Ham and Tottenham and while he scored regularly for the Hammers his career at Spurs was punctuated both by goals and bouts of controversy.

Kanoute moved to Sevilla in 2005 and has since helped the club win the Uefa Cup twice, the Uefa Super Cup, two Spanish cup competitions and earn a top three finish in La Liga with his goals coming at a rate of better than one every two games.

African footballer of the year in 2007, Kanoute enjoyed a successful 2007/08 Champions League campaign as his five goals helped Sevilla into the knock-out stages, where they lost to Fenerbahçe.

Did you know?

Manchester United's win over Chelsea on penalties was the ninth time the final of the competition (as either the European Cup or Champions League) has been decided on penalties.

Former Chelsea defender Celestine Babayaro is the youngest player to have appeared in the Champions League. He was 16 years and 87 days old when he played for Anderlecht against Steaua Bucharest in November 1994. It was certainly an unforgettable debut as he was also sent off!

Spain and Italy are the most successful countries in the competition with four wins each since the Champions League format was introduced in 1992/93.

Manchester United's 2008 Champions League success came 25 years after manager Alex Ferguson guided Aberdeen to European Cup Winners' Cup victory – a record time span for managers winning European trophies.

AC Milan boast the most Champions League final appearances with six. They also share the record number of wins with Real Madrid with three each.

The Moscow final was only the third time two teams from the same country have met in the Champions League final. Real Madrid beat Valencia 3-0 in 2000, while AC Milan defeated Juventus 3-2 in a penalty shoot-out in 2003.

Lazio goalkeeper Marco Ballotta is the oldest player to have played in the Champions League. He was 43 years and 252 days old when he faced Real Madrid in December, 2007.

Didier Drogba became only the second player to be sent off in a European Cup final when he was shown the red card in Moscow. Arsenal goalkeeper Jens Lehmann was the first when he was dismissed against Barcelona in 2006.

MOSCOW

FINAL

CHELSEA FOOTBALL CLUB

MANCHESTER UNITED

Champions League Maze

Answer on page 61

Montenegro to Manchester – Rangers' Story

When Rangers crashed out of the Champions League at the group stage, European glory might have been far from their minds.

But after re-grouping following the disappointment of missing out on the knock-out phase, the Glasgow club launched a remarkable Uefa Cup campaign that took them all the way to the 2008 final.

Walter Smith's side actually made an impressive start to their Champions League challenge, beating Stuttgart at home and then recording a magnificent 3-0 win away to French champions Lyon.

Ally McCoist and Nacho Novo salute the fans after defeat at the City of Manchester Stadium

Lee McCulloch, Daniel Cousin and DaMarcus Beasley scored the goals to record one of Rangers' best ever results in Europe and when they then drew 0-0 at home to Barcelona the Gers looked well placed in Group E to make the last-16.

Defeat in Barcelona followed and Rangers also lost away to Stuttgart but the other results meant that Smith's men knew a draw against Lyon in their final game at Ibrox would take them through.

Disastrously, though, they lost 3-0 with Jean-Claude Darcheville compounding a crucial miss by getting sent off.

However, there was consolation in the shape of a place in the Uefa Cup and Rangers certainly made the most of it.

Starting out in the last-32, they got past Panathinaikos on away goals thanks to a late goal in Greece by Nacho Novo with the kind of performance that was to become the hallmark of Rangers' run to the final.

Lee McCulloch in action against Werder Bremen in the UEFA Cup fourth round at Ibrox

Home goals from Cousin and Steven Davis in the next round gave Rangers an advantage over Werder Bremen which they did not relinquish as they reached the quarter-finals.

There they met Sporting Lisbon and after a goalless home leg turned in another superb away performance in Portugal with goals from Darcheville and Stevie Whittaker giving Rangers a 2-0 triumph and a place in a European semi-final for the first time in 36 years.

Serie A side Fiorentina stood in Rangers' way but nothing was to stop the Scots marching on as they showed remarkable courage to win through on penalties after both legs had finished 0-0.

Rangers hung on bravely in Italy after Cousin had been sent off to take the tie to spot-kicks and even though captain Barry Ferguson missed his effort, heroics from goalkeeper Neil Alexander and Nacho's clincher took them

through to the final at the City of Manchester Stadium to face Russian side Zenit St Petersburg, managed by ex-Gers boss Dick Advocaat.

Rangers fans converged on Manchester in their tens of thousands, hoping to see their side repeat their 1972 European Cup Winners' Cup success. Sadly for them Zenit proved too good as they secured a 2-0 win and Rangers suffered further disappointment when they lost out in the league title race to Celtic. But Smith's troops bounced back to win the Scottish Cup to add to their League Cup success and cap a memorable season.

Rangers celebrate victory over Fiorentina in the semi final in Florence

59

Chelsea's Colin Kazim Richards

Answers

WORDSEARCH SOLUTION

R	C	R	P	X	L	N	R	S	C	Z	Y	R
V	T	L	N	Y	Y	G	T	N	Z	S	V	C
Y	R	R	E	T	C	C	N	O	Z	E	G	Q
K	R	C	M	P	H	R	A	I	Z	I	N	G
W	G	N	E	E	H	W	L	P	X	T	W	L
Z	K	I	L	L	O	Q	I	M	K	L	C	I
N	G	S	G	C	T	T	M	A	N	A	R	V
F	E	K	S	G	H	I	B	H	P	N	O	E
A	Z	O	A	L	S	C	C	C	F	E	N	R
B	M	M	J	J	B	Z	E	Z	L	P	A	P
W	O	X	P	V	R	T	B	C	T	L	L	O
R	Y	B	A	R	C	E	L	O	N	A	D	O
F	E	R	G	U	S	O	N	Z	M	N	O	L

MAZE SOLUTION

QUIZ

1 Ronaldo

2 Barcelona

3 AC Milan, Real Madrid

4 Nicolas Anelka

5 Frank Lampard

6 Clarence Seedorf

7 Besiktas

8 Raul

9 Argentina

10 Didier Drogba

11 Colin Kazim Richards

12 Rangers